Make IT Now —
Bake IT Later! #1

Mostly Main Dishes
To be
Made in The Morning
Baked in The Evening
and
Served with Pride!

Grosset & Dunlap, Inc.
New York, NY 10010

Notes

Crab and Shrimp

Fit for an embassy buffet!

1 ½ pounds crabmeat
½ pound small shrimp
½ green pepper, chopped
⅓ cup parsley, chopped
2 cups cooked rice
1 ½ cups real mayonnaise
2 packages frozen peas, thawed
but not cooked
salt and pepper to taste

Toss lightly. Place in greased casserole. Refrigerate, covered.

Bake 1 hour at 350°, covered.

Serves 6

1

Notes

Greco

Inexpensive and different!

1 yellow onion, chopped
1 green pepper, chopped
1 or 2 small cans mushrooms, drained
2 cups shell macaroni
3 cans Tomato sauce
1 can cream style corn
   sharp cheese
1 pound ground round or chuck

Fry onion and green pepper in
   small amount of oil until glossy.
Brown ground meat in above. Keep
   moving to prevent burning.
Add mushrooms and remove from heat.
Boil macaroni until tender. Drain
   and add to above.
Add Tomato sauce and corn and
   mix all well.
Place in greased casserole and
   refrigerate.

when ready to bake, grate lots of
   sharp cheese on top and place
   in 300° oven for 1 hour.

Serves 6

2

Notes

Gnocchi

This is a really impressive, fluffy and
  smooth side dish for any roast. It
  can be served with gravy, or just
  butter.

2 cups milk, heated but <u>not boiling</u>
½ cup Cream of Wheat
1 Tsp. salt
¼ cup margarine, chopped
  dash cayenne
1 cup cheddar cheese, grated
1 egg, beaten with a fork.

Place warm milk, Cream of Wheat, salt,
  margarine, and cayenne in double
  boiler and heat thoroughly until
  margarine is all melted. Stir often.
Remove from fire - add grated cheese.
Add the egg. (I add 1 Tblsp. of the warm
  mixture to the egg and stir lightly.
  Then another Tblsp. and stir. Do this 5
  times, then add egg mixture to whole
  warm mixture. This way you will avoid
  danger of egg "stringing".)

Place in greased casserole and let stand
  at room temperature.

Bake at 350° for 1 hour until nice and
  brown on top.
If doubling (or more), decrease salt

Serves 4

3

Notes

Lobster Sturdevant

Serve this on a hot, sultry night in
shells or ramekins with a green
salad and corn pudding. It is just
right!

Cheese glass of real mayonnaise.
A little less than a cheese glass of
catsup.
½ jigger of chives (I cut them in
bits with scissors.)

½ cup lemon juice
Lots of paprika (about 1 Tsp.)
1 jigger brandy
1 pound prepared lobster or crabmeat

Mix and store in refrigerator.
Serve cold.

These are certainly unusual directions,
but it is the way it was told to
me, and I must say I would have a
hard time measuring ½ oz. of chives!

Serves 4

4

Notes

Spanish Bean Pot

A delicious new version of an old
favorite.

2 large (# 2½) cans red kidney beans
3 slices bacon
1 yellow onion
½ cup juice from can of peach halves
2 Tblsp. cider vinegar
¼ cup strong coffee

Drain beans, saving liquid.
Fry bacon and cut in small pieces.
Slice onion and fry in bacon grease.

Combine the above.

Then combine the following:
    1 clove garlic, grated
    1 pinch thyme
    1 pinch rosemary
    1 Tsp. salt
    1 bay leaf, broken
    2 Tsp. dry mustard
    ¼ Tsp. ground cloves
    ¼ Tsp. cayenne

Combine this second mixture
    with the first.   (cont'd)

Notes

Spanish Bean Pot (cont'd)

Place in greased casserole and refrigerate.

When ready to bake, place in very
slow oven 1 to 1½ hours.
Put 4 slices bacon on top the last
½ hour.
If it becomes too dry, add some
bean liquor.
Just before serving, add 1 jigger
brandy and stir casserole up
from the bottom to mix.

This can be made a day ahead,
baked when ready.

Peaches can be served as a side
dish with the beans.

If you double the recipe, do not
fully double the fruit juice
unless you want beans to
be very juicy!

Serves 6

Notes

Deviled Crab

This one can be prepared a day ahead, too!

1/4 cube butter
1 large onion, minced
2 stalks celery, chopped fine
1 1/2 pounds crabmeat, shredded
2 or 3 slices bread, toasted and crumbled fine
1 Tblsp. Worcestershire sauce
Dash cayenne
Salt and pepper
1/2 Tsp. dry mustard
mayonnaise

Fry onion and celery slowly in butter
until glossy. Remove from flame.
Add crab
Mix together the Worcestershire, cayenne,
salt, pepper, and mustard. Add to
crab mixture.
Add enough mayonnaise to hold together.
Refrigerate in shells or small individual
baking dishes.

When ready to bake, sprinkle with
crumbs, dot with butter, and place
in 400° - 450° oven for 15 minutes.

Serves 6-8

7

Notes

White Rice Browned

Our bachelor friend makes a whole meal
out of This!

1/2 cup butter or margarine
2 cups raw white rice
2 1/4 Tsp. salt
1/4 Tsp. pepper
2 cans beef consomme
2 cups water
1/2 cup chopped, blanched almonds (I prepare
    These ahead - or buy Them canned.)

Melt butter in large frying pan
Add rice
Cook over very slow fire, stirring often,
    until rice is golden brown.
Place in 2 qt. casserole.
Sprinkle on seasonings -

When ready To bake, add consomme,
    water, and nuts. Mix gently.
Cover and bake at 300° for 1 hour
    and 15 minutes. Do not stir.

Serves 10

Notes

Shrimp and Cheese Casserole

An all Time favorite! Serve This at your next party, and you will agree.

6 slices white bread
1 pound prepared shrimp (ready To eat)
1/2 pound Old English cheese (usually comes
    sliced)
1/4 cup margarine or butter, melted
1/2 Teasp. dry mustard - salt To Taste
3 whole eggs, beaten
1 pint milk

Break bread in pieces about size of a
    quarter.
Break cheese into bite size pieces.
Arrange shrimp, bread, and cheese in
    several layers in greased casserole.
Pour margarine or butter over This mixture.
Beat eggs. Add mustard and salt To eggs.
    Then add The milk. Mix Together
    and pour This over ingredients in
    casserole.
Let stand a minimum of 3 hours,
    preferably overnight in refrigerator,
    covered.

Bake one hour in 350° oven, covered.

Naturally if you slightly increase the
    amount of shrimp, you improve
    The dish - but it is fine "as is."
    When doubling The recipe, use
    3 pounds of shrimp.
                Serves 4

Notes

Stroganoff Bake

No last minute mixing in This Stroganoff.

6 slices bacon, cooked
2 pounds veal cut in large bite size pieces
2 large yellow onions, chopped
1/2 pound fresh mushrooms
1 pint commercial sour cream
1 cup white cooking wine
1 cup raw white rice

Set cooked bacon aside and brown veal
    in bacon grease. Remove from pan.
Brown onions in pan.
Slice mushrooms.
Combine veal, onions, and mushrooms,
    and add The sour cream which you
    have mixed with wine.
Cover and cook slowly on Top stove for
    2 hours. Stir occasionally.
Boil rice, drain, and combine with
    above mixTure in layers. Refrigerate.
When ready To bake, crumble cooked
    bacon on Top and bake, uncovered,
    at 300° for one hour or until
    piping hot.
Serves 6

10

Notes

Tomato Side Dish

Your friends will ask, "How did you make This?"

2 large cans solid pack Tomatoes
8 whole cloves
8 whole peppercorns
1 bay leaf (at least 1 inch long)
   salt
1/2 yellow onion, chopped
3/4 cup brown sugar
3 or 4 slices white bread pulled into
   dime size pieces.
2 Tblsp butter

Put cloves, peppercorns, and bay leaf
   in cheesecloth bag.
Cook Tomatoes, undrained, cheesecloth bag,
   and a dash of salt on Top of stove
   very slowly 30 minutes. Stir occasionally.
Add onion, sugar, bread, and butter.
Place in greased baking dish.

When ready To bake, remove cheesecloth
   bag and contents and bake at 400°
   1 hour.

Serves 6

Notes

Picnic Barbecue

When your relatives and all the children are coming, This is for you!

1 can corned beef, chopped
4 medium yellow onions, chopped
2 stalks celery, chopped
1 cup drained canned Tomatoes
1 1/2 cups water
1 Tblsp. chili powder
1 Tblsp. vinegar
3 Tblsp Worcestershire sauce
1/4 cup chili sauce

Saute onions and celery in a little oil until glossy.
Add all other ingredients and simmer very slowly, uncovered, 1 To 1 1/2 hours. Add a little more water if it becomes Too dry.

Reheat and serve in warm hamburger buns.

Serves 6

Notes

Chicken Supper Dish
Really deluxe!

6 full breasts of chicken, cooked
1 large yellow onion, chopped
1 cup raw white rice
1 #2 1/2 can solid pack Tomatoes, not drained
2 cloves garlic
2 small cans mushrooms, drained
1/2 green pepper, chopped

Simmer chicken until Tender. Save The broth.
Remove chicken from bones in large chunks.
Fry onions and green pepper in a little oil
   until glossy.
Add raw rice and keep over low flame until
   golden brown.
Add Tomatoes, garlic, mushrooms and
   simmer about 20 minutes. Remove
   garlic.
Place chicken in greased casserole and
   spread rice mixture on Top.
   Refrigerate after adding about
   one inch chicken broth To casserole.

Bake at 350° for 45 minutes. Add a little
   more broth if it seems dry.

Serves 6 generously

13

Notes

Crab and Spinach Casserole

Just right for luncheon or buffet supper.

2 pkgs. frozen chopped spinach
1 pound crabmeat
1 1/2 cups grated sharp cheese
1 cup finely chopped onions
1 can tomato paste
1 cup commercial sour cream
    dash nutmeg
    salt and pepper

Thaw spinach.
Grate cheese.
Start with layer of spinach, then
    onions, then crab, then cheese.
    Add nutmeg, salt, and pepper.
    Repeat once again. Refrigerate.
When ready to bake, put mixture
    of sour cream and tomato paste
    on top.
Bake 45 minutes in 325° oven.

Serves 4.

14

Notes

Noodles and Mushrooms

This is delicious with ham or any roast.

1 white onion
1 green pepper
½ cup salad oil
½ can cream style corn
1 can Tomato soup
1 box medium wide noodles
1 small can chopped or sliced ripe olives
1 small can mushrooms, drained
   grated cheese

Dice pepper and onions and fry slowly in
   oil until glossy.
Boil noodles 9 minutes.
Mix all ingredients Together (except cheese)
   and place in casserole. Refrigerate.

When ready To bake, cover Top with
   grated cheese. Place casserole in pan
   containing a small amount of warm
   water and bake at 350° for 1 hour.

If you wish To use iT as a main dish,
   brown 1 pound of ground round or
   chuck and add To casserole.

Notes

Sausage Casserole for Six

Your family will love this, and for company
 serve it with dry red wine, green salad,
 and French bread!

1 pound pork sausage (not highly seasoned)
½ green pepper, chopped
1 large can Tomatoes, mashed but not drained
6 bay leaves
 dash paprika
½ Tsp. Worcestershire sauce
1 pkg. fine noodles cooked in salted water
 Parmesan cheese

Crumble sausage and cook slowly until brown.
 Remove from pan and drain.
Saute green pepper in 2 Tblsp. oil or sausage
 fat until glossy.
Add all other ingredients to green pepper
 and simmer for 5 minutes, stirring
 occasionally.
Put all in greased casserole. Add salt
 and pepper if necessary.
Shake Parmesan cheese generously over top.
Refrigerate.

Bake uncovered 45 minutes at 350°
 until cheese is melted.
Serve with more Parmesan cheese.

Notes

Crab in Cups

Make a day ahead!

4 Tblsp butter, melted
4 Tblsp flour
1 Tsp wet mustard
1 Tsp salt
1 Tsp Worcestershire
Dash cayenne

1 cup canned Tomatoes, drained
1 cup mellow grated cheese
2 eggs, slightly beaten
1½ cups milk
2 cups crabmeat in chunks

Blend flour into melted butter. Add next seven
   ingredients. Cook slowly, stirring often,
   about 5 minutes or until cheese melts.

Heat milk
Add seasoned ingredients to milk.
Add crab.
Let thicken in top of double boiler. Stir
   occasionally. Refrigerate.

Reheat, uncovered, and serve in toast cups —
   with a little parsley and paprika on top.

Toast Cups

Rub muffin tins with margarine.
Decrust sliced bread. Push into cups.
Bake at 275° until golden brown.
Reheat on cookie sheet.

Serves 6

Notes

Mushrooms and Rice

I could eat this every night!

2 2/3 cups precooked rice
6 Tblsp. salad oil
2 small cans mushrooms, drained
  green onions, chopped
2 cans beef consomme, undiluted
2 Tblsp soya sauce
1/2 Tsp. salt

Mix and bake, covered, at 350° until
  water is absorbed, no more than
  30-45 minutes. Do not stir.

To prepare in advance, place dry
  ingredients in casserole and
  add liquids just before baking.

Serves 6

Notes

Rice and Deviled Eggs with Tuna

Deluxe and Inexpensive!

1/4 cup green pepper, chopped
1/4 cup minced onion
2 Tblsp. butter
1/2 cup milk
1 can mushroom soup
2 cups cooked rice
1 cup flaked Tuna
3/4 cup grated cheddar cheese
1 cup bread crumbs, fried slowly in butter
6 deviled eggs

Cook green pepper and onions in butter until glossy
Combine soup and milk
To 3/4 of the soup mixture, add rice and Tuna.
Place in casserole.
Top with deviled eggs and refrigerate.
when ready to bake, pour over remaining
     soup mixture and sprinkle with buttered
     crumbs and cheese.
Bake at 350° 40 minutes.

Deviled Eggs

6 eggs, hard boiled
1/2 Tsp salt, 1/8 Tsp. pepper, 1 Tsp. wet mustard,
     1 Tsp horse-radish
1 Tsp minced parsley
1/4 cup mayonnaise

Cut eggs in half lengthwise. Mash yolk. Add
     other ingredients to yolks and mix well.
Fill egg whites

Serves 6   19

Notes

Potato Casserole

A delicious potato dish using <u>canned</u> potatoes!

2 cans small white potatoes
parsley, chopped
pepper
Dill seed
Oregano
1 can mushroom soup
1 soup can of milk
garlic powder
paprika

Drain potatoes and place in baking dish.
Sprinkle generously with parsley.
Season with pepper.
Sprinkle with a pinch of dill seed.
Sprinkle with 2 pinches oregano, crumbled.
Dilute 1 can mushroom soup with 1 can milk.
Stir 1/8 Tsp. garlic powder into soup.
Pour this over potatoes.
Sprinkle paprika over top.

When ready to bake, place baking dish in 350° oven, covered, until hot — about 45 minutes.

Serves 4-6

Notes

Rice and Shrimp Casserole

An entirely differently flavored shrimp
   dish, and so good!

2 pounds shrimp - or 1 pound already cooked and
   prepared
⅓ cup onion, chopped and browned in
2 Tblsp. margarine
1 or 2 cloves minced garlic
1 cup raw white rice
1 large can Tomatoes, not drained
2 cups chicken bouillon
1 bay leaf broken in pieces
3 Tblsp. chopped parsley
½ Tsp. ground cloves
½ Tsp Marjoram
1 Tsp. chili powder
dash cayenne
1 Tsp salt
⅛ Tsp pepper

Combine onion, garlic, rice, bay leaf, parsley,
   cloves, marjoram, chili powder, cayenne,
   salt, and pepper in casserole. Mix gently.
Combine Tomatoes and bouillon.

Just before baking, add wet ingredients to
   dry, add shrimp, and mix!
Bake 1½ hours at 350°, covered.

Notes

Chicken Bake

My husband chuckled at this because to him "Half and Half" is a brand of Tobacco.

1 good sized fryer, cut in pieces
2 eggs, beaten
About 2 cups of flour seasoned with salt and pepper.
Margarine
1 cup "Half and Half" cream

Dip chicken pieces one by one in beaten eggs and then shake in paper bag containing the flour. Place in refrigerator covered with wax paper.

When ready to bake, lay side by side closely in baking dish or pan and dot with margarine. Add 2 slices of margarine to pan.

Place in 475° oven for 30 minutes. Tip the pan a time or two to spread the margarine on bottom of pan.

Pour Half and Half over chickens and bake 1 hour longer at 350°.

If chicken seems to be drying, you may add more Half and Half.

Be sure to let Half and Half reach room temperature, or it will crack a baking dish.

Serves 4

Notes

Green Rice

Perfect for a luncheon with salad.

3 cups cooked white rice
2½ cups milk
2 cups grated sharp cheese
2 eggs, beaten
2 Tsp. olive oil - or salad oil
1 cup chopped parsley
4 green onions, chopped fine
1 large Tsp. Worcestershire sauce

Mix all, season well with salt
and pepper, and place in
greased casserole.

When ready To bake, place in
350° oven for 45 minutes.

Serves 6

Notes

Crab Supreme

Make it a day ahead!

8 slices bread
2 cups crabmeat
1 yellow onion, chopped
1/2 cup mayonnaise
1 cup celery, chopped
1/2 cup green pepper, chopped

4 eggs, beaten
3 cups milk
1 cup canned mushroom soup
grated cheese
paprika

Cook celery slowly 10 minutes in a little water. Drain.

Dice half of bread into baking dish.

Mix crab, onion, mayonnaise, pepper, and celery and spread over bread.

Dice other slices of bread and place over crab mixture.

Mix eggs and milk together and pour over dish.

Cover and place in refrigerator overnight.

Bake for 15 minutes at 325° Then spoon soup over the top. Sprinkle top with cheese and paprika.

Bake one hour more or until golden brown.

Serves 8

24

Notes

Fried Rice

This really special casserole can be
made the main dish by adding shrimp,
chicken, ham, or Turkey.

2 Tblsp. salad oil
1 bunch green onions, chopped. (Include
    some of the green Tops.)
1 cup diced celery - or more
2 cups cooked rice
    salt
2 Tblsp. soya sauce (or 3 if you
    like it strong.)
    Chopped, blanched almonds, browned
        in butter

Saute onions and celery in oil but
    do not brown
Add rice (I use precooked rice), salt,
    and soya sauce.
Mix and place in casserole.

When ready To bake, place in 350°
    oven for ½ hour - or less - until
    thoroughly heated.
Toss almonds on Top just before
    serving.

Serves 4

25

Notes

Chicken Tamale

A real "company" dish!

3 Tamales cut into bite size pieces
    (or use 2 jars)
1 cup canned Tomato pulp (drain solid
    pack Tomatoes well)
1 small can whole Kernel corn
1 cup chopped or sliced olives (ripe)
½ cup chili sauce
1 Tblsp. olive or salad oil.
1 Tblsp. Worcestershire sauce
1 cup grated cheese
2 cups cooked chicken cut into
    good sized chunks (The equiva-
    lent of 1 large stew hen.)

Mix The above except cheese and
    store in casserole in refrigerator.

When ready To bake, cover with
    grated cheese and bake 1
    hour at 350°.

Serves 6 To 8

Notes

Quick Tamale

The family will love This

4 small cans chicken Tamale
2/3 can cream style corn
1/2 can pitted olives, drained (ripe)
1/3 cup grated cheese

Combine Tamale, corn, and olives.
Sprinkle cheese on Top.
Refrigerate

When ready To bake, place in
    350° oven, uncovered, for
    40 minutes.

Serves 4

Notes

The following are not
strictly "Baked Dishes";
however, They are The
"Frosting on The Cake"
and Too useful To be
omitted from a "Make IT
In Advance" cookbook!

Notes

Cranberry Salad Mold

2 cans jellied cranberry sauce
2 envelopes gelatine
1/2 cup cold water
1/2 Tsp. salt
2/3 cup chopped walnuts
2/3 cup diced apples
1/2 cup chopped celery

Crush sauce with a fork.
Put gelatine in water - let stand 2 minutes. (Do this in a small, flat bowl.) Place dish in pan of boiling water after gelatine is absorbed. Let stand until dissolved. Stir a bit.
Add gelatine to cranberry sauce and stir until smooth. Place in refrigerator for 1 or 2 hours until partially jelled.
Add remaining ingredients and pour into mold. Chill until firm.

Unmold when ready and pass mayonnaise when serving. Add a little red wine vinegar to mayonnaise if you want it more tart.

If made a day ahead, keep in refrigerator covered with aluminum foil.

Notes

Cream Dressing for Salads

1 pt. real mayonnaise
2 Tblsp. (generous) anchovy paste
3 Tblsp. Tarragon or red wine vinegar
1 Tblsp. scraped onion
1 small clove garlic, minced
6 fillet of anchovy, chopped
   (if you omit this, double the paste.)
1 Tblsp. chopped parsley
1 Tblsp. chives or green onion tops, cut
    fine

Mix vinegar with mayonnaise
Add other ingredients. Mix well.
Chill.

I serve this on a salad of only
   romaine lettuce.

If you yearn for a roquefort cream
dressing, just grate desired amount
of bleu cheese into dressing and mix
well. Omit all anchovy.

Can easily be made a day or so ahead.

Be sure to add all salad dressings
just before serving - and toss well.

Notes

My Favorite Dip

2 pkgs. cream cheese
2 beef bouillon cubes
   boiling water
   mayonnaise
5 green onions, minced
1/8 Tsp. Spice Islands Beau Monde
   Seasoning

Cream Together the cheese.
Dissolve bouillon cubes in smallest
   possible amount of water (about
   1/4 cup.) Add To cheese.
Add onion and Beau Monde.
Mix well and refrigerate.

When ready To serve, add mayonnaise and mix until dip is
   right consistency.

Notes

Potato Salad

4 cups diced, boiled potatoes
1 cup diced cucumber
3 Tblsp. minced onion
1 1/2 Tsp. salt
1/2 Tsp. pepper
3 hard boiled eggs, diced

Mix the above and toss with the following dressing:

Dressing

1 1/2 cups sour cream (commercial)
1/2 cup mayonnaise
1/4 cup vinegar
3/4 Tsp. celery seed
1 Tsp. wet mustard

Chill salad until ready to serve.

Serves 6 amply

Notes

My Favorite French Dressing

2 cups olive or salad oil
1/2 cup red wine vinegar, garlic flavor
2 Tsp. salt
2 Tsp. freshly ground pepper
2 Tsp. wet mustard
2 Tsp. Worcestershire sauce

Beat with an egg beater and store in refrigerator in covered container. If it separates, just let it stand for a while at room temperature.

Always shake well before using.

For Roquefort dressing, just add whatever amount of crumbled bleu cheese you like, and beat it along with rest of ingredients.

Add dressing to salad just before serving and toss well.

Notes

Pear Ring Mold

1 pkg. lime jello
canned pear halves
2 pkgs. cream cheese

Make lime jello according to directions on pkg.
Take half of it and pour over some canned
   pears in quart ring mold. Place in refrigerator to "set" a little. (1 or 2 hours)
Take other half of jello and add the cream
   cheese which has been put through a sieve.
Let this stand at room temperature until
   the first mixture has "set" partially.
Then pour jello-cheese mixture over jello-
   pear mixture and return mold to
   refrigerator to completely jell.

This can be served with 2 or 3 cups fresh
   grapes in center. Mix grapes into following sauce:
         2 egg yolks well beaten
         1 Tblsp sugar
         a little salt
         2 Tblsp. Tarragon vinegar
      Cook above in double boiler very care-
      fully until pretty thick. Chill, and
      when cold, add 1/2 pt. or less of
      whipped cream. Add grapes.
For the whole mold serve a dressing of
      mayonnaise with a little salad oil
      and lemon juice to taste added.   34

Notes

Dressing for Coleslaw

1/3 cup real mayonnaise

3 Tblsp. milk

1 or 2 Tblsp. pickle juice - depending
  on how tart you like it. (Use
  juice from sweet pickles, not dill.)

Minced green onion or green onion Tops

Mix mayonnaise and milk.

Stir in pickle juice.

Add onions.

Chill.

When ready To serve, add To 1
  pkg. fresh coleslaw or amount
  To serve 4. Toss well.

35

Notes

Pineapple - Cheese Salad Ring

½ pound cottage cheese
1 cup whipped cream
1 Tblsp. gelatine
½ cup water
2½ cups grated pineapple, drained
2 Tblsp mayonnaise
½ Tsp. salt

Rub cottage cheese through a
sieve. Add salt.
Soak gelatine in cold water and
dissolve over hot water.
Add cheese, mix well.
Add mayonnaise, pineapple, and cream.
Chill in ring until firm.

When ready, unmold and serve with
a dressing of mayonnaise plus a
little lemon juice and a little
whipped cream. Use fresh fruit in
center of ring.

36

Notes

Note

One half the author's profit from all six "Make It Now" books is given to:

The Cystic Fibrosis Foundation
6000 Executive Blvd.
Suite 309
Rockville, Md. 20852

If you would like a copy of any of the other "Make It Now" books, ask your local gift or bookstore or write for information to:

Barbara Goodfellow
409 First Street
Coronado, Calif. 92118

Notes

Notes

Notes

Notes

Notes